CW00493510

Foundations – Faith Life Essentials
Immersion In The Spirit

© 2011 Derek Prince Ministries–International
This edition DPM-UK 2020
ISBN 978-1-78263-548-2
Product Code: B105D

This message is a transcript book with questions and study suggestions added by the Derek Prince Ministries editorial team.

Derek Prince Ministries
www.derekprince.com

EXPANDED
VERSION:
**GROUP
STUDY**

Immersion
in the Spirit

DPM

DEREK PRINCE MINISTRIES - UK

Contents

About this Study Series 7

Immersion in the Spirit – an Introduction 12

Part 1 - Immersion in the Spirit 15

Part 2 - How the Holy Spirit Comes 37

Part 3 - Seven Requirements for Receiving 59

About the Author 67

About This Study Series

The Bible is God's Word and our "instruction manual" to find the path to salvation in Jesus. It then shows us how to walk with Him once we have come to know Him. Logically, therefore, it is a hugely important part of our challenge as Christian believers to study the Word of God.

A sad fact is that very often we forget most of what we have heard quite quickly! As a result, what we have heard often has little impact on the way that we continue to live.

That is why we developed these Study Guides. As Derek Prince has said numerous times in his teaching, "It is a general principle of educational psychology that children remember approximately 40 percent of what they hear; 60 percent of what they hear and see and 80 percent of what they hear, see and do."

This Study Guide is intended to help you to assimilate the truths that you have heard into both your head and into your heart so that they become more than just knowledge and will begin to change the way that you live.

Living the Christian life

This study is part of a series of 10 messages, based on the doctrinal foundation of the Christian Life described in Hebrews 6:1-2 which says,

Therefore, leaving the discussion of the elementary principles of Christ, let us go on to perfection, not laying again the foundation of repentance from dead works and of faith

toward God, of the doctrine of baptisms, of laying on of hands, of resurrection of the dead, and of eternal judgment.

This mentions six specific foundation stones that we need to lay before we can build a dwelling place for the Lord in our hearts and lives:

1. Repentance from dead works
2. Faith towards God
3. The doctrine of baptisms – John's baptism, Christian baptism and baptism in the Holy Spirit
4. Laying on of hands
5. Resurrection of the dead
6. Eternal judgment.

When this teaching is applied in your life, with faith, we believe that it will deepen your relationship with God and enable you to live a truly successful Christian life.

How to Study

Each book contains a QR-code (or DVD) that links you to a talk by Derek Prince, the transcript of the talk and questions for personal application or to be discussed in a group setting.

Each video is about an hour long, divided in three parts. Set aside a reasonable length of time to read the Introduction, then watch or read Derek's teaching, and finally come back to the Study Guide to reflect on the Study Questions or to discuss them with your study group.

Once you have completed this series you will find that you have an excellent summary of the teaching. This will help you to share the content with others, whether to a friend, home group or congregation. The more you share the truths you are learning, the more they will become part of your own life and testimony.

Group Study

This study guide has been developed for use by small groups as well as by individuals.

Simply proceed through the material as a team, reflect on the questions and explore the statements together for a rich and rewarding experience.

Scripture to Memorize

In this book, we have chosen key Scriptures for memorization. They will relate in some way to your overall study. Memorizing them will place a spiritual sword in your hands which you, by the Holy Spirit, will be able to use in times of spiritual conflict.

The Word of God has supernatural power for those who will take the time and effort to "hide it in their hearts" by memorizing and meditating on it. As God's Word is hidden in your heart, it becomes constantly available to you for reference, comfort, correction and meditation. Put simply, it becomes part of your life.

Look up the verse in your own Bible and write it in the space provided. You will want to write and say this verse out loud several times until you are confident you know it well. Take time to meditate on the words and their application to your life. As a group, you could talk briefly about the meaning of the verse and its relevance to the lesson or share how you applied it.

You will be asked to recall your Memory Work at the end of the book.

Immersion in the Spirit – an Introduction

The Bible shows there are three main baptisms which may be summarised as follows:

Type of Baptism	In what?	Into what?
John's baptism	Water	Repentance
Christian baptism	Water	Jesus Christ
Baptism in the Holy Spirit	Holy Spirit	One body – the Church

In this study, you will learn more about the baptism in the Holy Spirit. This baptism is essential if you want to live a strong Christian life. In the introduction to all four of the gospels (Matthew, Mark, Luke and John) it is stated that Jesus will baptize with the Holy Spirit. Did you realise that? Not only was Jesus to die in our place, but right in the beginning of His ministry it was announced that He would be the baptizer in the Spirit. This is very important to note – firstly because much of the Church seems to have overlooked it, but also because right from the beginning, God revealed how He will empower us to walk as Jesus walked.

In the title of this study, the word "Immersion" is used as a reminder of the true meaning of baptism as understood from the original Greek. The word itself is merely a transliteration of the Greek word *baptizo* meaning to dip or to immerse – either by going down into water, or by what Derek Prince calls the 'Niagara Falls experience' of being immersed from above.

Watch the Derek Prince video teaching *Immersion in the Spirit* on YouTube. Scan the QR-code or visit dpmuk.org/foundations.

This video has been divided into three sections, following the chapters in this book. You will find the links to these sections when you tap the 'down arrow' to expand the information about the video.

Write down these verses and try to memorize them.

Luke 11:13

Romans 6:13

God filled them;

but they began to speak.

The Holy Spirit did not

do the speaking; they did

the speaking while the

Holy Spirit gave them the

language.

Immersion in the Spirit

In the building of our Christian lives, Scripture lays out very plainly what comprises the foundation of our spiritual lives. In the construction of a building, the foundation is of paramount importance, because without an adequate foundation the size and stability of the building is limited. In the same way, it is important that we properly lay a foundation for our spiritual building.

We find the foundation doctrines of the Christian life in Hebrews 6:1–2:

> *Therefore, leaving the discussion of the elementary principles of Christ, let us go on to perfection, not laying again the foundation of repentance from dead works and of faith toward God, of the doctrine of baptisms, of laying on of hands, of resurrection of the dead, and of eternal judgment.*
> *Hebrews 6:1–2*

In this booklet we will continue our study of the third item in this list, "the doctrine of baptisms," and, in particular, how it relates to the baptism in the Holy Spirit.

By way of review of our previous study, the word *baptize* that we see in the Bible is not an English word. It is actually a transliteration of the Greek word *baptizo*. The meaning of this Greek word is absolutely beyond question: it means "to immerse."

I will be using the word immersion in this study to describe baptism, and in this case, immersion in the Holy Spirit.

As we studied previously, there are two ways of being immersed. There is the swimming pool way, where you go down into the water, go under the water and come up out of the water. That is like water baptism. Then there is the Niagara Falls way. The first time I stood and watched Niagara Falls, I said to myself, "You couldn't be under that waterfall one second without being totally drenched." That is like the baptism in the Holy Spirit.

Every place that the baptism in the Holy Spirit is described, it indicates in one way or another that the Holy Spirit came down over those receiving it from above. But in either case, you are totally immersed, not just partially immersed or sprinkled.

Jesus: the Baptizer

It is very interesting to note that the introduction to each of the four gospels specifically states that Jesus Christ would baptize in the Holy Spirit. I think far too little attention has been given to this fact.

In Matthew's gospel, John the Baptist says:

> *"I indeed baptize you with water unto repentance, but He who is coming after me* [the Messiah] *is mightier than I, whose sandals I am not worthy to carry. He will baptize you with the Holy Spirit and fire."*
> *Matthew 3:11*

In Mark, John the Baptist is speaking again:

> *"I indeed baptized you with water, but He will baptize you with the Holy Spirit." Mark 1:8*

In the account that is given in Luke's gospel, John the Baptist says this:

John answered, saying to all, "I indeed baptize you with water;
but One mightier than I is coming, whose sandal strap I am
not worthy to loose. He will baptize you with the Holy Spirit
and fire."
Luke 3:16

In John's gospel, this statement is included as part of the official introduction of Jesus by His forerunner, John the Baptist. In every one of the introductions in each of the four gospels, it is specifically stated that Jesus will baptize His people with the Holy Spirit. In John's gospel the introduction is a little fuller.

The next day John saw Jesus coming toward him, and said,
"Behold! The Lamb of God who takes away the sin of the
world! . . . I did not know Him, but He who sent me to baptize
with water said to me, 'Upon whom you see the Spirit [the
Holy Spirit] descending, and remaining on Him, this is He who
baptizes with the Holy Spirit.' And I have seen and testified
that this is the Son of God."
John 1:29, 33–34

John the Baptist says three things here: this is the Lamb of God; this is the Son of God; and this is He who baptizes in the Holy Spirit. We are all familiar with the statement that Jesus is the Lamb of God, but this is only stated in John's gospel, whereas in all four gospels it is specifically stated that Jesus is the Baptizer in the Holy Spirit. In other words, it is one of the most important things that we need to know about Him.

Of course, it is wonderful to know Jesus as Savior and to know Him as Lamb of God. But that is not the end. It is also very important that we come to know Him, individually and personally, as the Baptizer in the Holy Spirit. I cannot overemphasize how frequently this promise is given in the New Testament.

The Promise of the Spirit

After His earthly ministry was completed and after His resurrection, Jesus again states this promise:

> And being assembled together with them [the disciples], He
> [Jesus] commanded them not to depart from Jerusalem, but
> to wait for the Promise of the Father, "which," He said, "you have
> heard from Me; for John truly baptized with water, but you shall
> be baptized with the Holy Spirit not many days from now."
> Acts 1:4–5

Jesus was careful to repeat the promise with which John the Baptist had introduced Him—that He would be the Baptizer in the Holy Spirit.

Almost all commentators on the Bible agree that the fulfillment of this promise of Jesus is recorded in Acts 2:1–4, on the Day of Pentecost:

> When the Day of Pentecost had fully come, they were all with
> one accord in one place. And suddenly there came a sound
> from heaven, as of a rushing mighty wind, and it filled the
> whole house where they were sitting. Then there appeared
> to them divided tongues, as of fire, and one sat upon each of
> them. And they were all filled with the Holy Spirit and began
> to speak with other tongues [languages], as the Spirit gave
> them utterance [or gave them to speak].
> Acts 2:1–4

We see here three successive phases of that experience. First, it was a baptism. The Holy Spirit came from above and immersed them. The Holy Spirit filled the whole place where they were sitting, and they were immersed from above.

Second, each of them was individually filled with the Holy Spirit.

It was not just a collective experience, it was an experience in which each individual had his or her personal share.

Third, there was an overflow—a supernatural outflow from the infilling. This is in line with a principle stated by Jesus in Matthew 12:34, "For out of the abundance of the heart the mouth speaks." When a heart is filled, it overflows through the mouth in speech.

God's Part, Man's Part

There are a number of passages in the New Testament that speak about people being filled with the Holy Spirit. In each case, what followed their infilling was that the person prophesied, spoke in tongues, or glorified God in some way. It is a universal principle that when the heart is filled to overflowing, then the overflow takes place through the mouth in speech.

That is precisely what happened on the Day of Pentecost. When they had been filled, then they all began to speak with other languages as the Spirit "gave them utterance," or as the Spirit gave them the ability to speak. It is very important to understand that this is a matter in which God and man must cooperate. God filled them; but they began to speak. The Holy Spirit did not do the speaking; they did the speaking while the Holy Spirit gave them the language.

Because of my background in the Pentecostal and Charismatic movements, I have met so many who said, "Brother Prince, I want God to do it all." In one case, a man said, "I've been tarrying for twenty-five years. I'm waiting for God to do it all."

I replied, "That is not scriptural. God will do His part; but you have to do your part." We do the speaking; God gives the language. But God will not do the speaking. Remember, it says, "They all began to speak . . . as the Holy Spirit gave them utterance."

It is true: the disciples tarried, or waited, until the Holy Spirit came on the Day of Pentecost. They waited, however, because of Jesus' specific command to wait in Jerusalem until they had received the promise of the Holy Spirit which had not yet been given. (See Luke 24:49 and Acts 1:4–5.)

After that, there is no record that anyone ever tarried for the Holy Spirit. The Holy Spirit had been given and there was no need to wait. After Pentecost when they prayed and met the conditions, they immediately received the Holy Spirit.

If you meet the conditions, which we will consider later in this study, you can be filled with the Holy Spirit. If you have never received the Holy Spirit, this can be your opportunity.

A Seal and a Down Payment

The apostle Paul describes the infilling of the Holy Spirit as a seal:

Now He who establishes us with you in Christ and has anointed us is God, who also has sealed us and given us the Spirit in our hearts as a guarantee [deposit].
2 Corinthians 1:21–22

Paul tells us two things: the Holy Spirit is a seal and He is a deposit, or a down payment. In Ephesians, Paul uses similar language:

In whom [Jesus] also, having believed, you were sealed with the Holy Spirit of promise, who is the guarantee of our inheritance until the redemption of the purchased possession.
Ephesians 1:13–14

In the margin of the New King James Version for the word guarantee, it gives "down payment" as an alternate translation. Paul says the Holy Spirit is both a seal and a down payment.

First, the Holy Spirit is a seal. You already belong to Jesus, but this is a public identification that you belong to Him. He sets His public seal upon you.

There was once a day when a letter sent by registered mail had to be sealed with hot wax and then an imprint applied to the wax. In like manner, the Holy Spirit is a seal. He is a hot wax seal, and Jesus puts His imprint on it and His seal sets you apart. Just as registered mail is treated in a special way, when we have been baptized in the Holy Spirit, we get special attention from Heaven's post office.

The second term used in describing the Holy Spirit is down payment or deposit. The Greek word Paul uses is *arrabon*, which is derived directly from a Hebrew word.

In 1947, I was living in Jerusalem with my first wife, Lydia. We had just moved into a new house in Jerusalem and we needed to buy fabric for the curtains. We went to the Old City, found an Arab merchant who sold curtain material, and saw what we wanted. I do not remember the exact figures, so I will just say we needed twenty yards and the price was five dollars a yard which would make the total price one hundred dollars.

We said to the merchant, "We don't have all the money with us, but we'll give you twenty dollars as a down payment." In Arabic he called that *arbon*. Then we said, "Since we've given you the down payment, you have to remember two things: it belongs to us—you must set it aside for us and not sell it to anybody else; and, second, our down payment is our guarantee that we will come back with the rest of the money and take the material."

This is a parable of the baptism in the Holy Spirit. First, Jesus puts a down payment on us and sets us apart for Himself. After that, we are not for sale to any other customer.

Second, it is His guarantee that He is coming back to get us. And, when He comes back, we will be His forever. These are such brilliant, vivid pictures of the baptism in the Holy Spirit.

The Visible Sign

Exactly what is the visible seal of the Holy Spirit? In the New Testament the baptism in the Holy Spirit was both visible and audible. It is not merely something that happened inside the believers which could not be seen by others. It was both seen and heard.

This is a question that people might debate. But, as far as I am concerned, the New Testament only indicates one visible seal: speaking with other tongues as the Holy Spirit gives you to speak. This seal is visible, audible, and public.

A seal cannot be a secret, otherwise it does not accomplish its purpose. Acts 2:4 says the seal is, *"they . . . began to speak with other tongues* [languages], *as the Spirit gave them utterance* [to speak]."

There are cults (the Rastafarians in Jamaica, for example) where people speak in tongues. This frightens some people from seeking the baptism in the Holy Spirit, because they ask, "How do I know if I'm going to get the right thing?" In Luke 11:11, Jesus said that if a child asks his father for a fish He will not give him a snake. Then He adds:

> *"If you then, being evil, know how to give good gifts to your children, how much more will your heavenly Father give the Holy Spirit to those who ask Him?"*
> *verse 13*

In other words, if you are a child of God—and that is important to note—and you ask for the Holy Spirit, you have a written guarantee from God that you will receive the right thing. However, if you are not a child of God, this promise does not apply. You must be a child of God to receive the promise.

I believe that is why there are counterfeits. Individuals who have not been born into the Kingdom of God seek things in the spiritual realm and receive them—only they are gifts from darkness and not from God the Father. Jesus said very plainly, "If you ask your heavenly Father for the Holy Spirit, He will give it to you." You need not be afraid; your Father will give you what you ask for.

Facts about the Seal

Let's consider some facts about the seal as we have defined it—speaking in tongues.

First of all, it was the seal the apostles received in their own experience. Jesus said, "Behold, I send the Promise of My Father upon you; but tarry in the city of Jerusalem" (Luke 24:49). The disciples waited for ten days; then the Holy Spirit came and they spoke with tongues. This was the seal the disciples received in their own experience.

Second, it was the seal the disciples accepted in others—and we will examine one remarkable case in a moment.

Third, the disciples never asked for any other seal.

Over the years, many people have asked me, "How do I know if I've been baptized in the Holy Spirit? I've had this or that experience and I've been seeking God for an answer. How can I know for sure?"

My answer is, "You can know when you receive the seal. When you begin to speak with other tongues as the Spirit gives you to speak, you have it."

Let me add, we may speak of the baptism in the Holy Spirit as an "it," but in reality, you have "Him." The Holy Spirit is not an it, but a person you have received.

Those three facts again are:

1. It was the seal the apostles received.
2. It was the seal they accepted in others.
3. They never asked for any other seal.

Furthermore, the New Testament does not offer us any other seal. There is no alternative given.

Many people have said, "I got so happy. I was filled with joy. I was praising the Lord all the time. Isn't that the seal?" Not according to the New Testament. It is wonderful to be filled with joy and it is wonderful to be praising the Lord, but that is not the New Testament seal.

After the resurrection of Jesus, Luke's gospel records:

> He [Jesus] *was parted from them and carried up into heaven.*
> *And they worshiped Him, and returned to Jerusalem with*
> *great joy, and were continually in the temple praising and*
> *blessing God.*
> *Luke 24:51–53*

The disciples had great joy, they were continually praising and blessing God, but they had not yet received the seal. They did not receive the seal until the Day of Pentecost. Jesus told the disciples to tarry or wait until the promise came. And when the Holy Spirit came and they spoke with tongues, that was the end of waiting. They received the seal and they knew they had received the promise.

Gentiles Receive the Seal

There is one particular case in the book of Acts that demonstrates the seal so vividly. In Acts 10 is the account of how Peter had been supernaturally directed to the household of Cornelius. He never really wanted to go there because it was not permissible for him, as a Jew, to enter the house of a Gentile—much less to eat with one. However, under pressure from God, he went. And he took with him six other Jewish believers because he probably wanted to have witnesses. When he arrived, Peter preached to the Gentiles about Jesus and we read:

> *"To Him [Jesus] all the prophets witness that, through His name, whoever believes in Him will receive remission [forgiveness] of sins."*
> *Acts 10:43*

It is interesting to note how far Peter had come in his sermon. The people in the household of Cornelius simply believed and received forgiveness of sins. Once they had received forgiveness of sins, the Holy Spirit was prepared to come upon them. For then it says:

> *While Peter was still speaking these words, the Holy Spirit fell upon all those who heard the word. And those of the circumcision who believed* [the Jewish believers] *were astonished, as many as came with Peter, because the gift of the Holy Spirit had been poured out on the Gentiles also.*
> *verses 44–45*

The Jewish believers came to the house of Cornelius with Peter believing that the gospel was not for anybody but the Jews. They did not believe Gentiles could become believers. But when they heard them speak with tongues, they said, "They received the Holy Spirit just as we did. We can't argue with God." Why? "For they heard them speak with tongues and magnify God" (verse 46). They had no evidence other than the Gentiles speaking with tongues, and they asked for no other evidence. It was sufficient as a seal from God.

Fruit or Gift?

Some people today might have said, "We should wait for about six weeks to see if these Gentiles really bring forth fruit." However, the disciples did not wait; they didn't need to see fruit. Why? Because we are not talking about fruit, we are talking about a gift. They are two different matters, both very important. A gift is received in a single transaction; fruit comes by a slow process of growth.

Let me use this simple analogy. If you have a Christmas tree during the holiday season, you know that the gifts are placed under the Christmas tree. People for whom the gifts are designated gather around the tree and receive their gift. The gift is received by a single transaction; it is not a lengthy process.

Fruit, on the other hand, grows on a tree, perhaps an apple tree planted in your yard. But it will never grow on a Christmas tree. Fruit takes time to grow; it is a process.

Fruit is extremely important, but we cannot confuse fruit with a gift. We are talking about the gift of the Holy Spirit—something that can be received in one simple transaction.

Returning to the story, we read that Peter said to the rest of disciples,

> *"Can anyone forbid water, that these should not be baptized who have received the Holy Spirit just as we have?"*
> *verse 47*

Peter made no differentiation between these Gentiles and what happened to the disciples on the Day of Pentecost.

Later on, reporting to his fellow Jews who were criticizing him and complaining about him going to speak to the Gentiles, Peter said:

> *"As I began to speak, the Holy Spirit fell upon them, as upon*
> *us at the beginning."*
> *Acts 11:15*

There is no mention of a mighty wind or tongues of fire there in the household of Cornelius. The one manifestation that identified the experience was that they all began to speak with other tongues. I believe it cannot be questioned that this was the seal the apostles received, and this was the seal they accepted in others. They never asked for any other seal, and I cannot find any other seal offered in the New Testament.

The Stigma of Tongues

I am aware, probably more than most people, that speaking in tongues is sometimes considered strange and unorthodox—some people even call it demonic. There was once a dear evangelical minister who would not walk on the same side of the street with me because he knew I spoke in tongues. I forgave him, but I could not endorse his opinions.

Sometimes, at the beginning of a new experience that God is bringing to us, He puts a kind of stumbling block in our way. If we are not really in earnest about receiving what He is bringing to us, we will be put off. In regard to the baptism in the Holy Spirit, some people find it offensive to hear believers speaking a language they never learned, and maybe getting very excited about it.

I want to suggest that individuals like me from the Anglo-Saxon, European-American background have a false picture of what Christianity is really like. First of all, we think about it as being very dignified. When we get inside a church we do not speak in a loud voice. We stand or sit and sing the hymns, but we don't really get excited about anything. That is the picture of Christianity I grew up with. I went to church eight times a week for ten years as part of my educational process, so I am not without experience! However, this is not the biblical picture.

Many of us suffer because we are not really free to express what God is doing in us. When we read about the people in the Bible, we see that they cried, they shouted, they groaned, they clapped their hands, they danced, they sang, and they got excited. They were enthusiastic about God and knowing Him.

Are You Enthusiastic?

When I was the head of a college for training teachers in East Africa I had to hire the teachers. I learned that a teacher may have all the academic qualifications but not be much good as a teacher.

Another teacher with far less academic qualifications may be a much more successful teacher because of one thing—enthusiasm. I have come to the conclusion that there is no substitute for enthusiasm. Some years ago, when Ruth and I led a conference in Moscow, there were a thousand mostly new believers there and I was overwhelmed by their enthusiasm. I thought to myself, God, I wish I could find this in other places, too. When they started to sing, "Jesus Christ is Lord of all," they would go on singing for several minutes. Nobody had to work them up or conduct them. They just could not stop. I have a recording of that particular music and when I really need a lift in the spirit, I turn it on.

Though it is not a professional recording, what comes through is the excitement and enthusiasm. If you want other people to believe in what you believe, one of the best ways to convince them is to be enthusiastic. If you had suffered from corns and then found a remedy, you would be so excited you would want to tell everybody with corns that there was a remedy.

We have a much more valuable remedy than that. We have the remedy for sin. It is unnatural if we don't get excited and tell people about it. The One who provides the excitement is the Holy Spirit. We read in Romans:

> *Now may the God of hope fill you with all joy and peace in believing, that you may abound in hope by the power of the Holy Spirit.*
> *Romans 15:13*

What makes us "abound in hope"? The power of the Holy Spirit working in us fills us with hope. How many of us today are really abounding in hope? How many are excited about Jesus? How many of us are just bubbling over, so much so that we can't keep quiet? That is how we should be. All of this staid, dignified solemnity really does not have very much to do with the New Testament.

MY NOTES

Study Questions

1. What part of this study was new to you?

    ----

2. Share (or write down) your own experience in learning about the baptism in the Holy Spirit and speaking in tongues. What have you read, seen, heard or experienced? What questions does it raise? After writing or sharing your thoughts, take time to pray about it.

    ----

3. All four gospels give an account of the words of John the Baptist, stating that Jesus is the Baptizer in the Holy Spirit. Why would they put so much emphasis on this?

----

4. Read Matthew 12:34: Out of the abundance of the heart the mouth speaks. If you were to choose one word to describe what you spoke about today, what would it be? What is in your heart now? Have you already taken it to God in prayer? Take time to thank Him for His involvement!

----

5. Read 2 Corinthians 1:21-22 and Ephesians 1:13-14. The infilling of the Holy Spirit is described as a seal and a down payment. Describe in your own words what this means. What does this mean to you, personally, when applied to your situation or life?

----

6. According to Derek Prince, you have to be a child of God first, in order to receive the Holy Spirit. Why? How can anybody become a child of God?

----

7. Read Acts 10:43-45. Peter didn't believe Gentiles could become believers. Yet, he did proclaim the Gospel to them and they all believed. Is there someone, or a group of people, that you doubt will ever become a follower of Jesus? Write their name down. You might be thinking too small of God! Pray for boldness in your testimony and for the Holy Spirit to convince them.

----

8. Read Acts 10:47 and 11:15. Why was it important for Peter to hear Cornelius and his household speak in tongues?

    ----

9. A friend makes this statement to you: "Brother John claims to be baptized in the Holy Spirit; however, I don't believe it. He has none of the fruit of the Spirit in his life." How would you respond?

    ----

10. Derek Prince says: "We have the remedy for sin and we should be excited about it." Write down/share why this is such joyful news to you personally and to the world.

SUMMARY

- The fulfilment of the promise of the Holy Spirit is recorded in Acts 2:1-4. There are three distinct phases:
  - The baptism came from heaven and filled the whole house – they were immersed from above.
  - Each one of them was individually filled with the Holy Spirit.
  - There was an overflow, a supernatural outflow from the infilling. This accords with what Jesus says in Matthew 12:34: "...for out of the abundance of the heart the mouth speaks."

- Speaking in tongues is a matter in which God and man cooperate. God filled the disciples but they began to speak. The Holy Spirit didn't do the speaking; they did the speaking and the Holy Spirit gave them the language.

- Baptism in the Holy Spirit is a seal and a down payment.

- You have already chosen to follow Jesus but this publicly identifies you as belonging to Him. He sets His public seal upon you.

- Jesus puts a down payment on you and sets you apart for Himself. After that you are not for sale to any other customer.

- Baptism in the Holy Spirit is His guarantee. Jesus says "I'm coming back to take you. And when I come back, I'll come back with the rest of the payment and then you'll be mine forever."

The New Testament states
three reasons for the
baptism in the Holy Spirit:
to receive supernatural
power; for witness and for
service; and to produce
unity in the body of Christ.

How the Holy Spirit Comes

There are two ways that the baptism in the Holy Spirit is administered in the New Testament. One is directly from heaven; when it simply falls on people. On the Day of Pentecost and in the house of Cornelius the Holy Spirit sovereignly fell on people apart from any human instruments.

The other way the Holy Spirit comes is by the laying on of hands, which is described in three places. In Acts 8, we read about Peter and John in Samaria:

> *Now when the apostles who were at Jerusalem heard that Samaria had received the word of God, they sent Peter and John to them, who, when they had come down, prayed for them that they might receive the Holy Spirit. For as yet He [the Holy Spirit] had fallen upon none of them. They had only been baptized in the name of the Lord Jesus.*
> *Acts 8:14–16*

These people had heard the gospel preached by Philip. They believed and they had been baptized. This is clearly stated earlier in the same chapter. (See Acts 8:5.) They were saved, but they had not yet received the Holy Spirit. The apostles were not content with the fact that these people had been wonderfully saved. They wanted these new disciples to have the full measure of God's promise.

Then they [the apostles] *laid hands on them, and they
received the Holy Spirit.*
verse 17

In this instance, the Holy Spirit was ministered through the laying on of hands by other believers.

In Acts 9 we read how Saul of Tarsus (who became Paul) was in the city of Damascus after his confrontation with the Lord Jesus. A disciple named Ananias was sent to him, laid hands on him, and then prayed for him that he might be healed and receive the Holy Spirit. (See Acts 9:1–19.) Paul received the baptism in the Holy Spirit through the laying on of hands by Ananias.

In the third passage, Acts 19:1–7, Paul found certain disciples in the city of Ephesus. When he asked them if they had received the Holy Spirit when they believed, they said they had not even heard of the Holy Spirit. By their answer Paul knew they were not disciples of Jesus. He discovered they were disciples of John the Baptist. So he said, in effect, "That was all right in those days, but now you need to be baptized in faith in Jesus." Then they were baptized in water. Afterwards it says:

*And when Paul had laid hands on them, the Holy Spirit came
upon them, and they spoke with tongues and prophesied.*
Acts 19:6

Here again, the Holy Spirit came upon individuals through the laying on of hands and they spoke in tongues and prophesied. Let me suggest that far too many people are satisfied with just speaking with tongues after they receive the Holy Spirit. That is wonderful, but why not go on to prophesy?

I believe the Scripture indicates God intends all believers to prophesy as part of their experience. In 1 Corinthians 14:31, Paul says, "For you can all prophesy one by one." Too often we stop short of God's full intention.

Purposes of the Baptism

As I understand the New Testament, there are three stated reasons for the baptism in the Holy Spirit: to receive supernatural power; for witness and for service; and to produce unity in the body of Christ.

To Receive Supernatural Power

The primary purpose of the baptism in the Holy Spirit is to receive supernatural power from God. In Acts 1:8 we read how Jesus expressed this. He was about to leave His disciples, and these are His last recorded words on Earth. He said:

> *"But you shall receive power when the Holy Spirit has come upon you."*
> *Acts 1:8*

The word for "power" is *dunamis* in Greek, from which we get the English word "dynamite." Dynamite causes explosions. You will observe that when the Holy Spirit descended, it caused an explosion.

Many claim the disciples were empowered by the fact that Jesus had risen from the dead, but that is not accurate. Jesus had risen from the dead fifty days earlier, and no one in Jerusalem had heard about it. However, when the Holy Spirit came, all Jerusalem heard about it in a few hours. That was "dynamite"—it was an explosion.

Some people do not welcome explosions; they are frightened by them. If it is the Holy Spirit, I say, let Him explode! Let Him do whatever He wants. I have never hung from the chandeliers (as some folks say), but if that was what God wanted me to do, I would be happy to do it! We tend to be far too fearful of allowing the Holy Spirit to "explode."

For Witness and for Service

The disciples received the power to be witnesses.

> *"You shall receive power when the Holy Spirit has come upon you; and you shall be witnesses to Me."*
> *verse 8*

The message of the gospel is supernatural. It is not a record of natural events, but of events which are totally supernatural. Jesus died, He was buried and rose again, and He ascended into heaven. Those are supernatural events. If we are going to testify to supernatural events, we need supernatural power. Proper theology alone is not enough; we need to be empowered.

Sometimes sinners are more discerning than Christians. They know when the message comes with real supernatural power, and they will listen. I have discovered this in many different cultures where I have seen sinners discern the presence of supernatural power. It does something for them. It commands their attention. That is why Jesus said: "You shall receive power, and then you shall be witnesses to Me."

In Romans 15:18–19 Paul is speaking about his own ministry and he says:

> *For I will not dare to speak of any of those things which Christ has not accomplished through me, in word and deed, to make the Gentiles obedient—in mighty signs and wonders, by the power of the Spirit of God.*

Paul said that the only things worth talking about in his ministry were those which the Holy Spirit had done. He declared he would not even mention anything else because the Holy Spirit, by the supernatural power of signs and wonders, had made the Gentiles (the non-Jews, the unevangelized people) obedient.

I have dealt with Gentiles in many countries through the years but I think back especially to my five years in East Africa when I was principal of a college for training African teachers. At that time the ambition of every African was to get an education, thus our college was supplying something they desperately wanted. They would come to the college as students and they would be very cooperative and obedient, because they wanted an education. I remember one day calling the student body together and saying, "I want to thank you for your obedience and cooperation. Whatever we want you to do, you do it, because you want your education. But in the minds of most of you there is a question that has not been answered." That got their attention.

Then I said, "I can't tell you the answer to the question." Now I really had their attention. "The question is this: Is the Bible really a book for Africans, or is it just a white man's religion that doesn't work for Africans?" (That is exactly what their own elders were telling them.)

Finally I said, "You will never know the answer to that question until you experience the supernatural power of God in your life. When you do, you will know that it did not come from America or Britain. It came from heaven."

I continued to put the Word of God before them in the days that followed, but mainly I prayed. A few months later there was a sovereign, supernatural outpouring of the Holy Spirit on those students. Every student in the college was baptized in the Holy Spirit. Up to that time, we had to urge them to pray. From then on it was difficult to stop them from praying! They would spend half the night in their dormitories praying.

They had received the supernatural seal, the supernatural enduement with power from on high. My fellow white missionaries used to have the attitude (I am sorry to say this, but it was true): "You can only lift Africans so high spiritually; they won't go any higher." I did not argue with them, but I just spent time with the Africans. When the Holy Spirit fell, the missionaries came down to see what was going on. They suddenly discovered that Africans could go higher.

Those young men and women needed a supernatural experience of their own. It was not enough just to get a message from a person from another race and another culture.

In the next few months, among those students (most of them under the age of twenty-five) we saw all nine gifts of the Holy Spirit in operation. In fact, we also saw two people raised from the dead. People have sometimes asked me if I have ever seen anyone raised from the dead. I have! Believe me, when someone is raised from the dead, people sit up and listen!

Jesus said to His disciples, "As you go, preach, saying, 'The kingdom of heaven is at hand.' Heal the sick, cleanse the lepers, raise the dead, cast out demons" (Matthew 10:7–8). We need to bear in mind that Jesus never retracted that direction!

I have said to the Jewish people among whom I live: "We non-Jews owe an apology to you Jewish people for ever asking you to believe a gospel that was not supernaturally attested. Your whole background in the Scripture tells you that whenever God sends a message through a special messenger, in some way or another He always gives supernatural attestation."

That is really the purpose of the baptism in the Holy Spirit—to bring us into the realm of the supernatural, which is the only realm in which the gospel really can be effectively proclaimed.

In Hebrews 2 we read:

How shall we escape if we neglect so great a salvation, which at the first began to be spoken by the Lord, and was confirmed to us by those who heard Him, God also bearing witness both

with signs and wonders, with various miracles, and gifts of
the Holy Spirit, according to His own will?
Hebrews 2:3–4

The writer of Hebrews gives three reasons why we should attend to the gospel message. Number one, the first person who proclaimed it was Jesus. Second, it was confirmed by those who were personal eyewitnesses of Jesus. However, the third reason is the Holy Spirit bears supernatural testimony to the message with signs, wonders, and gifts of the Holy Spirit.

The unbelieving world has a right to expect the supernatural from the Church along with its witness. We are living below the level of the will of God if we just present an intellectual message and quote a few Scriptures. Some people will get saved, and that is wonderful, but it is not God's best. Our witness for Jesus should be accompanied by the supernatural power of the Holy Spirit.

Baptized into One Body

One further reason for the gift of the baptism in the Holy Spirit is stated in 1 Corinthians 12:13. This is one of the most misunderstood verses in the whole of the New Testament. Actually, it is mistranslated and that is because the translators had a preconception of what they thought Paul was trying to say. The New King James Version that I use and most of the other translations read the same:

For by one Spirit we were all baptized into one body—whether
Jews or Greeks, whether slaves or free—and have all been
made to drink into one Spirit.
1 Corinthians 12:13

The mistranslated word here is "by," because in the Greek it says "in one Spirit we were all baptized into one body." There is no suggestion anywhere else in the New Testament that the Holy Spirit baptizes people. People are baptized in the Holy Spirit, but the Holy Spirit does not baptize. We are born again of the Holy Spirit—that is what brings us into the body.

The word emphasized in this passage is the word one. Paul is saying that the purpose of the baptism is to produce unity in the body. In one Spirit we were all baptized into one body—and we are all given to drink of one Spirit. Three times he uses the word one.

I pointed out in our previous study with regard to the use of the word baptize, that when you are baptized, you are baptized in something and baptized into something.

The "New Testament Baptisms" chart that follows makes this distinction clear.

In both John's baptism and Christian baptism, those being baptized were already in what they were baptized "into."

New Testament Baptisms			
Baptism	Requirements to receive	Element of baptism (IN)	New position or state (INTO)
John the Baptist	Repentance Confession of sin Evidence of repentance	Water	Forgiveness of sins
Christian / water	Hear the gospel Repent Believe Good conscience	Water	Christ Newness of life
Holy Spirit	Repent Be baptized Be thirsty Come to Jesus Ask Receive/drink Yield	Holy Spirit	Body of Christ

John's baptism was a baptism of repentance, but he would not baptize anyone who had not already repented. The baptism of John did not produce repentance. It was John's acknowledgment that a person had repented.

In Christian baptism (baptism in water), we are baptized into Christ. However, at the time we are water baptized, we are already in Christ, because we have heard the gospel and believed. Otherwise we have no right to be baptized. Being baptized in water does not put us in Christ; rather, it seals us as having been in Christ already. It is the same with the baptism in the Holy Spirit: "In one Spirit we were all baptized into one body." This does not mean we were not in the body, but that this is the seal that we are already in the body.

In every baptism, we have "baptize in" and "baptize into." "In" is the medium in which we are baptized. With John's baptism the medium was water and with Christian baptism the medium is water. With the baptism in the Holy Spirit the medium is the Holy Spirit.

What we are baptized "into" is what we are already in, but it marks us out as being in this new state or position: in repentance, in Christ, and in one body.

Paul's point in 1 Corinthians 12:13 is that the Holy Spirit is designed to produce unity in the body. Unfortunately (and this is one of the tragedies of recent Church history), the Church has been so self-serving and fleshly minded that instead of accepting unity, we have often used the baptism in the Holy Spirit to produce division. For this, all of us need to repent.

The baptism in the Holy Spirit is designed to make us know that we are part of one body and that every other true believer, no matter what denomination or what race or what culture, is a member of the same body. There is only one Holy Spirit and there is only one body. The unity of the body of Christ is God's purpose. Unfortunately, like so many other things, we have abused God's purpose.

Unity, Not Division

In similar fashion, the celebration of communion was designed to emphasize the unity of the body. What have we done through our carnality? We have allowed the communion celebration to divide us. That is not God's fault, it is ours. All of us need to bear some responsibility for how we have fostered division in the body of Christ.

For example, the non-Charismatics have been critical while the Pentecostal/Charismatics have been arrogant. I was a Pentecostal long enough to know that our famous slogan was, "We've got it all." However, when I looked at some of them, I thought, whatever you have, it isn't much! This arrogance has offended many people and caused them to miss the blessing of God.

Although we, as Charismatics, may have the "full gospel," we don't have more than what we have appropriated by God's grace. We may have the baptism and speak in tongues but still be very short of God's standard. Because we have the baptism in the Holy Spirit it is no guarantee that we are perfect or mature. Rather than being a seal of perfection, the baptism in the Holy Spirit is a help for us to become mature.

Many Spirit-filled Christians have the attitude that because they are saved, born again, baptized in water, and speak in tongues that they have arrived. Rather, the fact is they have just gotten started! The baptism in the Holy Spirit is not the goal but the gateway. If we treat the gateway as the goal, we will never get any further.

Some of us need to give heed to that. It is our carnality that divides us, but the baptism in the Holy Spirit is to bring Christians into unity.

Physical Manifestations

The physical manifestations that often accompany the baptism in the Holy Spirit can be controversial and we need to consider them. It is my opinion that most Christians are living what I call "bottled up lives." They are not free to express what God has put in them because there is a standard of dignity: to speak with a quiet voice, not get too excited, and sit upright in the pew. When we are in church, we stand up, sit down, kneel down, stand up, and then walk out of church!

Such behavior, however, has very little to do with New Testament Christianity. As a matter of fact, it has very little to do with the experience of people in the Bible, most of whom got excited. As you read the psalms of David you see that he roared, he cried, he drenched his couch with his tears. He was a man of strong emotion. Even Jesus groaned and wept; He expressed His feelings.

No one has more background in this than I do. I was brought up in Britain at the very center of the "old school tie" tradition, which meant you attended the most exclusive and prestigious schools in the land.

I was educated in Eton and Cambridge; I was a bastion of the Empire. As such, I regularly attended services of the Church of England which were "British" in every sense of the word: dignified, unemotional and solemn. However, one night in an army barrack room during World War II, God baptized me in the Holy Spirit. I was so ignorant at the time that I didn't know you had to go to church to get saved or be baptized in the Spirit. I received both of them in an army barrack room in the middle of the night.

Most of us, because of cultural training, have quenched our emotions. We have not given free expression to what God has done in us. Real worship is not just saying words; it is an attitude of the entire body. The scriptural picture of worship is bending down, kneeling, lying prostrate and clapping hands.

We have fallen far short of the standards of the Bible, and one main reason is that we have not expressed what the Holy Spirit has put in us. We have quenched or suppressed the Spirit. We have tried to be dignified because we thought it was the proper thing to do. We have been afraid of being too emotional or excited. I emphasize this as we approach the subject of physical manifestations because our backgrounds have taken us so far away from what the Scripture presents as normal.

Biblical Examples

Here is a short list of people from the Bible who have met God, including how they responded physically:

Abraham. The Lord appeared to him, and what did Abraham do? He fell on his face. (See Genesis 17:1–3.) How many of us would do that? I often smile when I hear Christians singing the hymn, "All hail the power of Jesus' name, let angels prostrate fall." Those dear church members think it is all right for angels to fall, but not them. They are much too dignified for that!

Israel. When the Lord accepted their sacrifice with supernatural fire, they all fell on their faces and shouted. (See Leviticus 9:24.) They did not use hushed speech. The Bible says in many places, "Let us shout joyfully." (See Psalms 66:1; 88:1; 95:1–2.)

Please understand, shouting is not singing aloud. Shouting is shouting! Some of you undoubtedly go to football matches or watch them on television. When your team scores a goal, what do you do? You stand up and shout! Why? Because you are excited. If you can get excited about football, why not get excited about Jesus and the Holy Spirit?

Joshua. He met the Commander of the army of the Lord outside Jericho and he fell flat on his face. (See Joshua 5:14.) I would venture to say that most of the great men of the Bible have been on their faces before God at least once.

Then God said to Joshua, "Take your sandal off your foot, for the place where you stand is holy." I have been in a place where people were moved to take off their shoes. Once, in a conference in Jerusalem, God moved in, and without anybody being instructed, everyone just quietly began to slip their shoes off their feet because they knew they were in a holy place.

The priests. When the fire of God, the presence and glory of God, came into the temple, the priests fell on their faces because they could no longer stand. (See 2 Chronicles 5:14.)

Jeremiah. I like to read Jeremiah because he was a respectable prophet. Consider his physical reaction to the presence of the Lord.

My heart within me is broken because of the prophets [the false prophets]; all my bones shake. I am like a drunken man, and like a man whom wine has overcome, because of the Lord, and because of His holy words.
Jeremiah 23:9

Jeremiah's reaction to the holiness of the Lord was very physical. He said, "All my bones shake." Your bones cannot shake without your whole body shaking. Jeremiah said, "I am like a drunken man because of the holiness of the Lord." It is possible to sense the holiness of the Lord in such a way that it impacts your entire physical body. Unfortunately, most of us are living on a very low level when it comes to experiencing the power of the Holy Spirit! The apostles. On the Day of Pentecost when the Holy Spirit came, the apostles behaved in a very strange, undignified way. (See Acts 2:13.) They were all speaking together in languages they had never heard. What did the unbelievers say? "They're drunk!" Have they ever said that about you when you walked out of church?

John the apostle. He encountered Jesus in a vision and he fell at His feet as one dead. (See Revelation 1:17.) There was a power that overwhelmed him so that he could not continue to stand.

Often when the Holy Spirit comes with power, I have seen people fall down, lie on the floor for extended periods of time, shake, dance with joy, cry, and laugh. However, because of their religious backgrounds, people often become fearful or are put off by such behavior. We need to expand our freedom in the Holy Spirit to make room for Him to bring our whole bodies into our experience with the Lord.

Study Questions

1. If you were to recall one or two things from this study that really stood out for you, what were they?

    ----

2. Read Acts 2:1-4, Acts 10:44-47, Acts 8:14–19, Acts 9:17, and Acts 19:6. Describe the two ways people receive the Holy Spirit. Would this still be the same today? Why (or why not)?

    ----

3. Is it possible for somebody to be saved without having received the Holy Spirit? Why or why not? (See Acts 9:1-18, Acts 19:1-7)

----

4. Reflect on Acts 8:14-17. Why did the apostles pray for the believers and lay hands on them to receive the Holy Spirit, even though they had been saved by their faith in Jesus?

----

5. How would you respond to someone who said, "I have received the baptism in the Holy Spirit, but the Lord has not yet given me the gift of tongues"?

----

6. The baptism in the Holy Spirit may be accompanied by physical reactions. Some people are held back from receiving the Holy Spirit because of these manifestations, yet God wants all of us to receive the Holy Spirit. Why?

    ----

7. Read Acts 4: 23-31 and Ephesians 6: 19-20. We need to be baptized in the Holy Spirit in order to effectively proclaim the Gospel. Take time to pray for all those who share the gospel – missionaries, pastors, Bible school students, evangelists, youth leaders, and yourself, for a fresh infilling of the Spirit and for God to supernaturally confirm their testimony.

    ----

8. According to the language of the Bible, when you are baptized, you are baptized *in* something and baptized *into* something. Explain this in your own words.

---

9. The Holy Spirit baptizes us into one body. Why could this unity be so important to God?

---

10. Derek Prince stated that: "the doctrine on the baptism in the Holy Spirit has been a cause for division in the Church. All of us need to bear some responsibility for how we have fostered division in the body of Christ. All of us need to repent. It is our carnality that divides us." Would you agree? If so, what does it mean to repent in this regard, what does repentance look like?

---

11. Reflect on how people responded physically to God: falling on their face, shouting, taking off their shoes, shaking, and speaking in tongues. Can you give examples of how people respond to God's presence in our time, or in your church?

SUMMARY

- Baptism in the Holy Spirit is not the goal, it is a gateway. It is not the end point but rather the start of a new, Spirit-empowered life in Christ.

- The overall purpose of the baptism in the Holy Spirit is to receive supernatural power from God (Acts 1:8). In particular, there are two over-arching purposes for this power:
  - For witness and service – If we are going to testify to the supernatural events of the gospel, we need supernatural power. (see also Romans 15:18–19, 1 Corinthians 2:1–5, Hebrews 2:3–4)
  - To make the unity of the body effective. (1 Corinthians 12:13)

- According to 1 Corinthians 12:13 believers are baptized in the Holy Spirit and into one body. The body refers to the body of Jesus which is one of the names for the Church. Jesus is the head and we are the body – baptism in the Holy Spirit puts a seal on that position.

You do not receive the
Holy Spirit by praying;
you receive the Holy Spirit
by drinking.

3

Seven Requirements
for Receiving

There are seven requirements for receiving the baptism in the Holy Spirit. It is important to understand these in order to fully receive what God has for us.

1. Repent. "Repent . . . be baptized" (Acts 2:38).
2. Be baptized. "Be baptized . . . and you shall receive the Holy Spirit" (Acts 2:38).
3. Be thirsty. Jesus said, "If any man thirsts, let him come to Me and drink" *(John 7:37–38)*.
4. Come to Jesus. There is only one Baptizer in the Holy Spirit. If you want the baptism, you have to come to the Baptizer.
5. Ask. Jesus said, "If you then, being evil, know how to give good gifts to your children, how much more will your heavenly Father give the Holy Spirit to those who ask Him!" (Luke 11:13). A lot of Christians say, "If God wants me to have the Holy Spirit, I guess He'll give it to me. I don't need to ask." However, Jesus said you do need to ask. Your heavenly Father will give the Holy Spirit to those who ask.
6. Receive/drink. Receiving is compared to drinking (See Acts 8:14–15; John 7:37.)
7. Yield. This is the difficult part for some people. You have to yield the unruly member of your body—the member which you often cannot control—the tongue. The control of the tongue by the Holy Spirit is God's evidence that He has come in to take control.

In the Bible the tongue is called "my glory." Not all translations are worded this way, but in Psalm 16:9 the psalmist said, "Therefore my heart is glad, and my glory rejoices." Peter quoted that psalm in Acts 2:26 saying, "Therefore my heart rejoiced, and my tongue was glad."

Our tongue is our glory because we are given a tongue for one supreme purpose: to glorify God. Any use of the tongue that does not glorify God is a misuse. When the Holy Spirit comes and takes control of the tongue, everything we say will glorify God. This may be the first time we are really using our tongues for the purpose for which God put a tongue in our mouths.

Are You Thirsty?

We have come to the end of the teaching and we now need to consider the application. As you are reading this you may begin to realize that you are thirsty. I would like to tell you very simply how you can receive the Holy Spirit right now.

Jesus said:

> *"If anyone thirsts, let him come to Me and drink. He who believes in Me, as the Scripture has said, out of his heart [actually, "his belly"] will flow rivers of living water." But this He spoke concerning the Spirit, whom those believing in Him would receive; for the Holy Spirit was not yet given, because Jesus was not yet glorified.*
> *John 7:37–39*

The Holy Spirit could not be given until Jesus was glorified. But when He was at the Father's right hand, Jesus poured out the Holy Spirit.

The conditions I have listed are very simple. You may or may not have met all these conditions. I want to emphasize that these guidelines help us enter into the fullest experience in the Holy Spirit. But Jesus is the Baptizer, and He is in control.

You may not have been baptized. I was not baptized when God filled me with the Holy Spirit because I did not even know about being baptized. The Gentiles at the home of Cornelius were not baptized.

There are, however, certain basic conditions which, I believe, Jesus clearly stated in this passage, "If anyone thirsts, let him come to Me and drink." Then He says, "out of his belly will flow the rivers." What a marvelous, supernatural transformation! You come as a thirsty person and become a channel of rivers of water. Being thirsty simply means we earnestly desire the Holy Spirit.

What must you do? It is very simple: Jesus said, "Come to Me." There is only one Baptizer, who is Jesus, and we come to Him to receive the baptism.

Next you need to drink. This is where religious people have a problem. It is just too simple. No one ever drank with their mouth closed and no one ever received the baptism in the Holy Spirit with their mouth closed. You drink by opening your mouth and breathing in the Holy Spirit. You are not taking in water, but you are breathing in the supernatural power of God. I have seen as many as three thousand people receive in one experience—but they all drank.

After the drinking, there is the overflow. Remember, "Out of the abundance of the heart the mouth speaks" (Matthew 12:34). This is where you have to have faith, because the Holy Spirit is not going to do the speaking for you. You must speak as the Holy Spirit gives you words. This is a step of faith, but "without faith it is impossible to please [God]" (Hebrews 11:6).

When Jesus baptized me in Holy Spirit, I had this strange sensation in my belly. I thought, what is this? The phrase came to my mind "speaking with other tongues." I thought, what's this got to do with speaking with other tongues?

Then I said out loud to God in an empty room, "God, if you want me to speak with tongues, I'm ready to do it." Then a sensation moved up through my chest and into my throat and my tongue started to move. I knew I was not controlling it, and the next thing I discovered, I was speaking a language somewhat like Chinese. I was ready to yield to God and the Holy Spirit provided the words. I believe God moved my tongue for me, because I was ignorant of the fact that I needed to cooperate with Him in this matter.

Do You Want to Receive?

If you would like to receive this wonderful, supernatural experience, I will give you a very simple prayer that you can pray by which you will present yourself to Jesus as a candidate for the baptism. You will come to Him, ask, and then drink. This is the point where religion makes it difficult because you have to do something simple and practical that might look silly. You need to open your mouth and begin to drink in the Holy Spirit. It is not water, but it is the Spirit of God that you are drinking in.

After a little while, that little mouthful you take in turns into a river and it starts to flow out through your mouth. Wherever you are, just shut yourself in with God; don't bother about your surroundings. Remember this crucial step: you drink (breathe in), and then at a certain point you begin to speak in faith. As a child of God, if you ask for bread He will never give you a stone. If you ask for the Holy Spirit, the Holy Spirit is what you will get.

The first part of the prayer is a confession of your faith in Jesus as your Savior. If you have never been saved, you can be saved right now as you pray. Then you qualify to receive the Holy Spirit. Please read this prayer out loud so you can hear yourself pray. When you say "amen" at the end of this prayer, don't pray anymore because you have asked Jesus to baptize you in the Holy Spirit and He has done it.

You do not receive the Holy Spirit by praying; you receive the Holy Spirit by drinking. A lot of people have prayed themselves right out of it because while you are speaking in your own language, you cannot speak another language. You have to stop speaking English and begin to speak your new language.

Please remember you are praying to Jesus. I am just giving you the words with which you can come to Jesus. When you have said, "Amen," you begin to drink.

PRAYER

Lord Jesus Christ, I believe that You are the Son of God and the only way to God. I believe that You died on the cross for my sins and rose again from the dead. I confess any sins I have committed and I trust You to forgive me and to cleanse me in Your precious blood. I thank You for doing this.

Now, Lord Jesus, I come to You as my Baptizer in the Holy Spirit. I open myself up to You and I ask you to baptize me in the Holy Spirit. Now, I begin to drink of Your Spirit that You are already pouring out on me. [Drink deeply by faith.]

I trust You, Lord, to give me the overflow. In faith, I thank You for this now. In Your name, Jesus. Amen.

Now, breathe in deeply, begin to yield your tongue and then begin to speak. You need to speak just clearly enough to know you have spoken in a new tongue. Take time to enjoy the Lord. Forget your problems, your questions, and just let yourself go. Release yourself to the Lord through this experience.

If you have difficulty, remember that Jesus asked Peter to step out of his little boat and walk on the water. Peter had to step out of the boat and walk. Jesus would not do that for him. There was nothing supernatural about Peter walking; he did it every day of his life. Peter walked and the power of God kept him from sinking. Likewise, if you yield your tongue to the Holy Spirit in faith, He will supply the words, but you must begin to speak.

Now, thank the Lord Jesus for this precious gift. If you get a little excited, it is understandable. Once you begin to speak in this new language, you are communicating directly with the Lord. The Holy Spirit is praying through you directly to the Lord. (See 1 Corinthians 14:2.) He no longer has to go through the bottleneck of your narrow little mind because your spirit is free to communicate with God.

Don't stop with a single experience. Make speaking in tongues a regular part of your daily experience and this precious gift of God will become more fluent and abundant as you yield yourself to Him.

What This Gift Will Do

It is important to understand what the Bible says about speaking in tongues. As you grow in this gift bear certain things in mind.

First, Paul said, "If I pray in a tongue, my spirit prays, but my understanding [mind] is unfruitful" (1 Corinthians 14:14). If you do not understand the words coming out of your mouth or if they sound silly, that is normal. Paul said our minds will not understand. It is your spirit that is praying, not your mind. Your mind is used to being in control of your words and it may seem strange when it is not included.

Second, speaking in tongues builds us up. Paul said, "He who speaks in a tongue edifies [builds up, strengthens] himself" (1 Corinthians 14:4).

Third, when we speak, or pray, in tongues we are speaking directly to God (1 Corinthians 14:2). Praying in tongues is a direct link to God that bypasses all the complications of our own thoughts and desires. When we pray in tongues, we can be assured that we are praying the will of God.

The Bible says, "Behold, God will not cast away the blameless [or "perfect man," KJV] . . . He will yet fill your mouth with laughing, and your lips with rejoicing [shouting for joy]" (Job 8:20–21).

MY NOTES

Study Questions

1. Discuss/reflect: is the Baptism in the Holy Spirit a separate experience from salvation or is it received automatically at the time of salvation?

    ----

2. To what degree should we trust our emotions as evidence of being in a right relationship with God? Or *not* being in a right relationship with God?

    ----

3. Why would the Scripture consider the tongue to be the most unruly member of our body?

-----

4. Derek Prince lists seven requirements for receiving the Holy Spirit. Write them down and reflect on them; have you met each of them?

-----

5. Do you want to receive the Holy Spirit? Earlier in this study, Derek Prince suggested that Christians sometimes stop short of God's full intention. Do you personally long to receive the fullness of God's Spirit or is something holding you back? Pray about this.

-----

6. Why is speaking in tongues a step of faith? Ask God for boldness to overcome anything that is withholding you from taking this step and from receiving what God the Father wants you to receive – His Spirit.

----

7. Read Luke 11:11. Some people seeking the Baptism in the Holy Spirit are frightened they will receive an evil, demonic spirit. What could cause this fear? How would you answer them?

----

8. Derek Prince encourages believers to make speaking in tongues a regular part of their daily experience with God. For what reason?

As you finish this study, ask for God's help to apply the truths from this study practically in your life. Remember to thank God for every new revelation that He shows you and to receive it with gladness.

Suggestion for prayer

Pray for you to develop a greater thirst for the power of the Holy Spirit.

If you haven't already received the baptism of the Holy Spirit, then review the seven conditions to make sure you have fulfilled each one and listen again to the part where Derek Prince leads the audience into receiving the Holy Spirit which is the best way because you can be listening and focussing on Jesus rather than needing to read.

Alternatively, you can simply pray the same prayer below:

PRAYER

Lord Jesus Christ, I believe that You are the Son of God and the only way to God, that You died on the cross for my sins and rose again from the dead. I confess any sins I've committed and I trust You to forgive me and to cleanse me in Your precious blood. I thank you for doing this. Now, Lord Jesus, I come to You as my baptizer in the Holy Spirit. I open myself up to You and I begin to drink of Your Spirit that You are already pouring out on me. Amen.

Now yield your tongue and begin to speak clearly enough to know that you have begun to speak in tongues. Forget your problems and your questions and release yourself to the Lord through this experience. Continue speaking in tongues, all the while thanking God in your mind for His wonderful gift which will empower you to live victoriously through Jesus.

SUMMARY

- The Bible reveals seven requirements for receiving the baptism of the Holy Spirit.
  - Acts 2:38 indicates the first two requirements which are key in preparing the people to receive the Holy Spirit:
  - Repent – make a firm decision to have a change of mind and a change of direction.
  - Be baptized.

  In John 7:37-38, Jesus stood and cried out, "If anyone thirsts, let him come to Me and drink." The following three requirements are all found in this verse:
  - Be thirsty – The word "if" shows us that this is a condition that we must fulfil.
  - Come to Jesus - There is only one baptizer in the Holy Spirit and if you want the baptism you need to come to Him.
  - Drink - this is compared to receiving and is an active participation in the process. God does not force His Holy Spirit on those who are not willing.

  The last two are:
  - Ask God the Father – Luke 11:13 says: "If you then, being evil, know how to give good gifts to your children, how much more will your heavenly Father give the Holy Spirit to those who ask Him!"
  - Yield your tongue - The control of the tongue by the Holy Spirit through the gift of tongues is the evidence that He's come in to take control (see Romans 6:13).

In the next study, *Transmitting God's Power*, you will discover the biblical doctrine of laying on of hands. By it, Christians may transmit God's blessing and authority and commission someone for service.

*Recall and write down the verses you memorized
at the beginning of this book:*

Luke 11:13

Romans 6:13

About the Author

Derek Prince (1915–2003) was born in India of British parents. He was educated as a scholar of Greek and Latin at Eton College and King's College, Cambridge in England. Upon graduation he held a fellowship (equivalent to a professorship) in Ancient and Modern Philosophy at King's College. Prince also studied Hebrew, Aramaic, and modern languages at Cambridge and the Hebrew University in Jerusalem. As a student, he was a philosopher and self-proclaimed agnostic.

Bible Teacher

While in the British Medical Corps during World War II, Prince began to study the Bible as a philosophical work. Converted through a powerful encounter with Jesus Christ, he was baptized in the Holy Spirit a few days later. Out of this encounter, he formed two conclusions: first, that Jesus Christ is alive; second, that the Bible is a true, relevant, up-to-date book. These conclusions altered the whole course of his life, which he then devoted to studying and teaching the Bible as the Word of God.

Discharged from the army in Jerusalem in 1945, he married Lydia Christensen, founder of a children's home there. Upon their marriage, he immediately became father to Lydia's eight adopted daughters – six Jewish, one Palestinian Arab, and one English. Together, the family saw the rebirth of the state of Israel in 1948. In the late 1950s, they adopted another daughter while Prince was serving as principal of a teacher training college in Kenya.

In 1963, the Princes immigrated to the United States and pastored a church in Seattle. In 1973, Prince became one of the founders of Intercessors for America. His book Shaping History through Prayer and

Fasting has awakened Christians around the world to their responsibility to pray for their governments. Many consider underground translations of the book as instrumental in the fall of communist regimes in the USSR, East Germany, and Czechoslovakia.

Lydia Prince died in 1975, and Prince married Ruth Baker (a single mother to three adopted children) in 1978. He met his second wife, like his first wife, while she was serving the Lord in Jerusalem. Ruth died in December 1998 in Jerusalem, where they had lived since 1981.

Teaching, Preaching and Broadcasting

Until a few years before his own death in 2003 at the age of eighty-eight, Prince persisted in the ministry God had called him to as he traveled the world, imparting God's revealed truth, praying for the sick and afflicted, and sharing his prophetic insights into world events in the light of Scripture. Internationally recognized as a Bible scholar and spiritual patriarch, Derek Prince established a teaching ministry that spanned six continents and more than sixty years.

He is the author of more than fifty books, six hundred audio teachings, and one hundred video teachings, many of which have been translated and published in more than one hundred languages.

He pioneered teaching on such groundbreaking themes as generational curses, the biblical significance of Israel, and demonology. Prince's radio program, which began in 1979, has been translated into more than a dozen languages and continues to touch lives. Derek's main gift of explaining the Bible and its teaching in a clear and simple way has helped build a foundation of faith in millions of lives. His nondenominational, nonsectarian approach has made his teaching equally relevant and helpful to people from all racial and religious backgrounds, and his teaching is estimated to have reached more than half the globe.

DPM Worldwide Ministry

In 2002, he said, "It is my desire – and I believe the Lord's desire – that this ministry continue the work, which God began through me over sixty years ago, until Jesus returns." Derek Prince Ministries International continues to reach out to believers in over 140 countries with Derek's teaching, fulfilling the mandate to keep on "until Jesus returns." This is accomplished through the outreaches of more than thirty Derek Prince offices around the world, including primary work in Australia, Canada, China, France, Germany, the Netherlands, New Zealand, Norway, Russia, South Africa, Switzerland, the United Kingdom, and the United States.

For current information about these and other worldwide locations, visit **www.derekprince.com.**

FOUNDATIONS
faith life essentials

www.dpmuk.org/shop

This book is part of a series of 10 studies on the foundations of the Christian faith.

Order the other books to get everything you need to develop a strong, balanced, Spirit-filled life!

1. Founded on the Rock

There is only one foundation strong enough for the Christian life, and we must be sure our lives are built on Jesus Himself.

2. Authority and Power of God's Word

Both the Bible and Jesus Christ are identified as the Word of God. Learn how Jesus endorsed the authority of Scripture and how to use God's Word as a two-edged sword yourself.

3. Through Repentance to Faith

What is faith? And how can you develop it? It starts with repentance: to change the way we think and to begin acting accordingly.

4. Faith and Works

Many Christians live in a kind of twilight - halfway between law and grace. They do not know which is which nor how to avail themselves of God's grace.

5. The Doctrine of Baptisms

A baptism is a transition - out of an old way of living into a totally new way of living. All of our being is involved. This study explains the baptism of John and the Christian (water) baptism. The baptism in the Holy Spirit is explained in 'Immersion in the Spirit'.

6. Immersion in the Spirit

Immersion can be accomplished in two ways: the swimming pool way and the Niagara Falls way. This book takes a closer look at the Niagara Falls experience, which relates to the baptism of the Holy Spirit.

7. Transmitting God's Power

Laying on of hands is one of the basic tenets of the Christian faith. By it, we may transmit God's blessing and authority and commission someone for service. Discover this Biblical doctrine!

8. At The End of Time

In this study, Derek Prince reveals the nature of eternity and outlines what lies ahead in the realm of end-time events.

9. Resurrection of the Body

The death and resurrection of Jesus produced a change in the universe. Derek explains here how the resurrection of Jesus impacted man's spirit, soul, and body.

10. Final Judgment

This book examines the four major, successive scenes of judgment in eternity. Exploring the distinctive aspects of these four judgments, Derek opens the Scriptures to bring forth treasures hidden there.

Christian Foundations Course

If you have enjoyed this study and would like to deepen your knowledge of God's Word and apply the teaching – why not enrol on Derek Prince's Christian Foundations Bible Course?

Building on the Foundations of God's Word

A detailed study of the six essential doctrines of Christianity found in Hebrews 6:1-2.

- Scripture-based curriculum
- Practical, personal application
- Systematic Scripture memorisation
- Opportunity for questions and personal feedback from course tutor
- Certificate upon completion
- Modular based syllabus
- Set your own pace
- Affordable
- Based on *Foundational Truths for Christian Living.*

For a prospectus, application form and pricing information, please visit www.dpmuk.org, call 01462 492100 or send an e-mail to enquiries@dpmuk.org

Foundational Truths
For Christian Living

Develop a strong, balanced, Spirit-filled life, by discovering the foundations of faith: salvation; baptism, the Holy Spirit, laying on hands, the believers' resurrection and eternal judgment.

Its reader-friendly format includes a comprehensive index of topics and a complete index of Scripture verses used in the book.

ISBN 978-1-908594-82-2
Paperback and eBook
£ 13.99

www.dpmuk.org/shop

More best-sellers by Derek Prince

- Blessing or Curse: You can Choose
- Bought with Blood
- Life-Changing Spiritual Power
- Marriage Covenant
- Prayers & Proclamations
- Self-Study Bible Course
- Shaping History Through Prayer and Fasting
- Spiritual Warfare for the End Times
- They Shall Expel Demons
- Who is the Holy Spirit?

For more titles: www.dpmuk.org/shop

Inspired by Derek's teaching?

Help make it available to others!

If you have been inspired and blessed by this Derek Prince resource you can help make it available to a spiritually hungry believer in other countries, such as China, the Middle East, India, Africa or Russia.

Even a small gift from you will ensure that that a pastor, Bible college student or a believer elsewhere in the world receives a free copy of a Derek Prince resource in their own language.

**Donate now: www.dpmuk.org/give
or visit www.derekprince.com**

Derek Prince Ministries

DPM–Asia/Pacific
38 Hawdon Street
Sydenham
Christchurch 8023
New Zealand
T: + 64 3 366 4443
E: admin@dpm.co.nz
W: www.dpm.co.nz

DPM–Australia
15 Park Road
Seven Hills
New South Wales 2147
Australia
T: +61 2 9838 7778
E: enquiries@au.derekprince.com
W: www.derekprince.com.au

DPM–Canada
P. O. Box 8354
Halifax
Nova Scotia B3K 5M1
Canada
T: + 1 902 443 9577
E: enquiries.dpm@eastlink.ca
W: www.derekprince.org

DPM–France
B.P. 31, Route d'Oupia
34210 Olonzac
France
T: + 33 468 913872
E: info@derekprince.fr
W: www.derekprince.fr

DPM–Germany
Söldenhofstr. 10
83308 Trostberg
Germany
T: + 49 8621 64146
E: ibl@ibl-dpm.net
W: www.ibl-dpm.net

DPM-Netherlands
Nijverheidsweg 12
7005 BJ, Doetinchem
Netherlands
T: +31 251-255044
E: info@derekprince.nl
W: www.derekprince.nl

Offices Worldwide

DPM–Norway
P. O. Box 129
Lodderfjord
N-5881 Bergen
Norway
T: +47 928 39855
E: xpress@dpskandinavia.com
W: www.derekprince.no

Derek Prince Publications Pte. Ltd.
P. O. Box 2046
Robinson Road Post Office
Singapore 904046
T: + 65 6392 1812
E: dpmchina@singnet.com.sg
W: www.dpmchina.org (English)
       www.ygmweb.org (Chinese)

DPM–South Africa
P. O. Box 33367
Glenstantia
0010 Pretoria
South Africa
T: +27 12 348 9537
E: enquiries@derekprince.co.za
W: www.derekprince.co.za

DPM–Switzerland
Alpenblick 8
CH-8934 Knonau
Switzerland
T: + 41 44 768 25 06
E: dpm-ch@ibl-dpm.net
W: www.ibl-dpm.net

DPM–UK
PO Box 393
Hitchin SG5 9EU
United Kingdom
T: + 44 1462 492100
E: enquiries@dpmuk.org
W: www.dpmuk.org

DPM–USA
P. O. Box 19501
Charlotte NC 28219
USA
T: + 1 704 357 3556
E: ContactUs@derekprince.org
W: www.derekprince.org